FLOWER CHILD NOIR

poems by

Deborah Kaufman

Finishing Line Press
Georgetown, Kentucky

FLOWER CHILD NOIR

Copyright © 2023 by Deborah Kaufman
ISBN 979-8-88838-129-8 First Edition
All rights reserved under International and Pan-American Copyright Conventions. No part of this book may be reproduced in any manner whatsoever without written permission from the publisher, except in the case of brief quotations embodied in critical articles and reviews.

ACKNOWLEDGMENTS

"A Father's Work," "Gloria," and "Vienna" were previously published in *Multiplicity Literary Magazine*.

Gratitude to my teachers at The Writing Salon, especially Brian Tierney whose incisive criticism and insight have helped shape this work.

Appreciation to readers Susan Griffin and Constance Hale, and to those who have cheered me on—Leanna James Blackwell, Alexa Dvorson, Nancy Fishman, Adam Hirsch, Mollie Katzen, Micha Peled, Janis Plotkin, and my much-missed sisters - Sharon Kaufman and Ann Snitow.

Most of all, thanks to my family—especially my mother Shirley Kaufman and my father Bernard Kaufman Jr. whose voices I hear in my dreams—and to my compañeras: Fatosh Arabacioglu, Tania Chelnov-Snitow, Sarah Hendlish, Marlese Kaufman, Lisa Hirsch Marin, Samia Van Hattum, Taslim Van Hattum, Fatima Van Hattum, and Rabia Van Hattum.
And to Alan Snitow, always.

Publisher: Leah Huete de Maines
Editor: Christen Kincaid
Cover Art: Kaufman family collection
Author Photo: Alan Snitow
Cover Design: Elizabeth Maines McCleavy

Order online: www.finishinglinepress.com
also available on amazon.com

Author inquiries and mail orders:
Finishing Line Press
P. O. Box 1626
Georgetown, Kentucky 40324
U. S. A.

Table of Contents

West Portal
A Father's Work 1
Gloria 2
Nightmares 4
Old Folks Land 5
The Great Parade 6
Road Trip 7
Dinner Parties 8
The World Got Sad 9
Shame 10
Vienna 12
Beth Sholom 13
West Portal 15
Gun in the Closet 17
One Martini Please 18
Girl Scouts 19
Forest Hill Station 7:00am 20
Red Skateboard 21

Urban Renewal
Urban Renewal 25
Human Be In 26
Zig Zags 27
The Poet's Party 28
Literary Agent 29
Mom On Fire 30
News 32
Denise 33
Name Changes 34
Shoplifter 35
The Back Room 37
War of Attrition 38
We Board the 6 Masonic 39

Deep Red World

Privilege 43
Cathy 45
The Boys from the Haight 46
N Judah to the Surf.. 47
Om Shanti... 48
Home Improvement... 49
They Shoot Horses, Don't They? 50
Laura 51
Mt. Lassen... 52
Steady 53
Kelly Girl... 54
Mug Shot 55
Dream of the Stormy Petrel... 56
Divorce 57

Homecoming

Sisters 63
Homecoming 64
October War... 66
Jealous 67
Phantom 68
Braids 69
The Land of Forgetfulness... 71
On Her Desk 72
Purple Heels 73
Return 75
After the End of the World... 76
Formica Table... 77
Burial 79

Notes 80
About the Author 81

West Portal

A Father's Work

He'd disappear early
with a black leather bag
bulging with stethoscope, bandages, morphine,
an inheritance from his father, the country doctor.
Silent, though his spine throbbed
as he shuffled down the stairs to his car
into the cold to do hospital rounds
in corridors mopped clean with disinfectant,
and the curtained cubicles where patients lay
with IVs and thin blankets and feeble smiles,
thinking maybe he'd get the nurse to up the narcotics.
In the doctor's lounge,
coffee in a Styrofoam cup
then on to his store-front office
where the waiting room was crammed with old men
and neighborhood drunks, biding time on frayed chairs.
After dark he'd go on house calls,
mostly to the ones in dirty bathrobes
who chewed tobacco and smelled like pee
and had strange stories to tell.
Late at night we'd hear the garage door open
gather around as he ate warmed up meat on a chipped plate
telling us about the heartbeat,
the gin under the bed, the color of their fingernails,
making us guess the diagnosis.
It was a running competition between sisters
desperate for his attention.
He'd peel an orange with steely precision
as we three girls chirped 'heart attack,'
'stroke,' or 'overdose,'
hoping to win his approval.
And mom stood, back to us all,
water running at the sink,
cleaning pots with steel wool,
scouring until her knuckles were white.

Gloria

She was the quiet one
an only child
lived with her immigrant family
in the back rooms of their deli
on West Portal Avenue.
Behind the glass shelf
salamis and strange cheeses
were laid out in broken spirals,
like the journey her parents had taken
escaping terror.
My mother referred to it in code
something about camps
I didn't understand.
Each week, we made a pilgrimage to the Lido Delicatessen,
past Toy Village, the Manor Coffee Shop,
and the produce store where the Italian guy flirted
with all the housewives.

At Halloween our school chose teams
to paint holiday pictures on shop windows.
Gloria and I were assigned Shaw's
popular ice cream parlor and candy store
down the street from their deli,
with its red and white awning, smell of fudge
butter brickle, and candied cherries.
We hatched the idea together
the Devil and Dracula,
blood dripping from their fangs
heads the size of the whole storefront window
scars and bloodshot eyes
mostly black and red
a stark contrast to the other childrens'
happy pumpkins, cats and spider webs.
We won a prize for artistic merit
not for the dread and horror
of her family's secret story
which we'd drawn on the glass.

And then we had our picture taken
holding hands
in front of the terrible truth.

Nightmares

I had nightmares of a blood-red
mushroom cloud I saw once
on the cover of the Dell paperback
my father crammed on the bookshelf
between Graham Greene and Albert Einstein,
bold script screaming *Survive an Atomic Attack!*

He had the whole family load
canned provisions into a basement shelter—
tuna fish and sliced Cling peaches
stacked in rows on the cement floor
below ground, like shell casings,
smell of car oil seeping in from the garage
where he parked each night,
coming home late from hospital rounds,
a Bowie knife in the glove compartment
ever since he'd been mugged
outside the Emergency Room—

fixed blade with a wooden handle,
a veteran's protection from his own nightmares:
D-Day and Buchenwald
and the patient with a Nazi tattoo under his arm.
Fear pulsed through my father's veins
with such velocity
it spilled like a tsunami
into our living room
where I sat with
my nuclear terror.

Old Folks Land

Friday dinner on Yesterday Street—
immigrant grandparents, the old apartment house,
bleached stucco, terra cotta tiles,
Otis elevator with a shaky metal gate.
On the way up, my little fingers
poke through accordion doors.
In the kitchen, Josephine stirs soup,
one eye peering through a milky cataract.
Steam, heaps of potatoes, cloves of garlic,
the whole place smelling like Silesia and dusty books.
I squirm at the table through three courses of boredom,
then carouse with older cousins, jump on a swollen sofa
in the back room with its worn red rug.
My sticky fingers carelessly open Poppie's prized album—
under cellophane, stamps neatly pressed,
Vienna, Melbourne, Hong Kong,
pelicans, gondolas, foreign alphabets
and typeface the width of a silken hair.
An atlas of perforations and pale watermarks,
the old country they left resting heavy in my arms.
Hal and Lynne and Joanie, tired of these faded dream-worlds,
throw meaty grapes out the window
onto people and cars below.
When they hit their targets they shriek with glee.
The sticky splats on windshields and cement
look like crushed bugs
or inkblots the shape of Poland.

The Great Parade

After the accident
when she slipped and broke her hip,
after they implanted a steel pin inside
to hold the bones together,
and after she won a lawsuit
against the department store,
mom packed our bags,
took us to the city of glass
and vertical certainty. We woke
to a steam heater's inexorable clanking,
rode an elevator up the deco high-rise
past silver gargoyles to the observation deck,
wind in our teeth, silk scarves flapping
as we smiled for the camera,
mom with her carmine lipstick
and a peculiar look of delight.
Racing uptown in a checkered cab,
we were the cheerful pistons and
industrial cylinders of *Ballet Mécanique*,
human gears entering the spiral shell tower,
kinetic, euphoric, finally arriving
at *The Great Parade*—the clown and horse,
umbrella and banjo, the man with the green hat!
I was a dizzy sprite, six stories high,
scampering around the curly-cue ramp,
imagining myself inside Legér's pageant,
with his acrobats and that blazing blue ribbon
sailing across the sea of canvas.
Mom wandered after me, limping a little
along the gentle incline, calling out my name
inside the white nautilus.

Road Trip

We're in the back seat
driving down 99
father at the wheel
telling a fantastical story—
the black oil spots on the road
are the footprints of wandering Roma
as they dance down the highway each night.
If only we could see them.
In no hurry, we cross over to 101,
wave to kids in passing cars,
count mirages in the shimmering heat.
At San Juan Bautista there is a rest stop;
we sit in the shade of the Pepper trees
eating peaches, fingers sticky with juice.
A little bronze plaque in the corner
of the overgrown cemetery
remembers the Amah Mutsun
buried here at the Mission,
thousands of slaves, and kidnapped children.
"Children like us?" we ask,
the sweet fruit nectar
dripping like blood
into the soil beneath our feet.

Dinner Parties

Dark magic was simmering,
merry copper pots, their lids akimbo,
Mickey Mouse with his broom
in the *Sorcerer's Apprentice*
before things got out of control.
Mom was in the steamy kitchen
wearing a flimsy stained apron
tied tight at the waist.
When the sky turned purple,
she emerged from her cookhouse chrysalis
in an emerald silk dress,
a smudge of *Chanel* on her wrists.
The doorbell rang,
a menagerie tumbled in,
women with voluptuous décolletage
reached towards platters of hors d'oeuvres,
and bourbon over ice.
I was sent in pink pajamas to watch tv
wrapped in a chenille blanket
faintly smelling of smoke.
Through the closed door, curled on a couch,
I heard the confusing repartee of grown-ups,
the clinking of plates and glasses.
After dessert, they'd sit on upholstered couches,
mom lighting Dutch cigarillos
plucked from a small tin box,
the guests tittering until late at night.
I fell asleep on an island of stuffed animals,
little expatriate beyond the border,
set apart from their secrets,
dad with his covert affairs,
stack of *Playboys* hidden beneath
a sea of socks in the dresser drawer,
mom smoking pot somewhere else
with the men who wore leather.

The World Got Sad

On my stomach,
propped on elbows,
urchin on a pea green rug,
skimming National Geographic,
full page ads for Buick
and Breck, maps of Nigeria,
pictures of the Queen.
The den is a medley,
Greenfields and *Sloop John B,*
Dad's cherry tobacco in a Meerschaum pipe,
mom opening the wooly sofa-bed
where we curl up together
to watch *Peter Pan.*
Those sterling days when Pete the Greek
came with his toolkit and miniature poodle,
fiddled with the tv antenna,
whistling *You Are My Sunshine*
smelling of whiskey and ash.
I climbed all over him in childish play
like I did with the cheerful milkman
who came to the side door,
and Chester the handyman
who cleaned the fireplace,
and sipped from a bottle
when he went down to the basement
before mom fired him and the world got sad.

Shame

I had a red *Crayola*,
a magic wand held
in the palm of my doughy hand.
Alone in the living room,
I crept along the four walls
under the frames of oil paintings
drawing huge circles—
moons, halos, crowns,
seventeen of them at eye level
until my parents walked in
horrified, and I felt
the hot thrum of their anger.
My father lifted me, threw me down
onto his lap and flopped on the couch.
It wasn't the seventeen hard spanks
on my naked rear that made me scream.
It was that my two older sisters ran in
to watch the show, my body scarlet
while they stood quietly by.
A degradation, primordial,
but only a hint of my father's first humiliation—
escaping terror as a boy,
crossing the Austrian frontier
with his Jewish scout troupe,
evading police. Penniless,
they hitched a ride on a garbage barge
downstream to Venice,
were stranded for days on the bare floor
of a *signora's* dismal garret.
Starving, the older boys chose my father,
the youngest, to beg for food.
He thrust his trembling hand through barbed wire
into the Hotel Excelsior's lavish
beachside restaurant.
The tables were crowded.
A fat man in a dark suit rose, grinning,
walked slowly towards him, bent down,

threw a heap of scalding sand
into my father's face.
What he remembered most
was the laughter and his skin
burning.

Vienna

After the Imperial Palace
five of us in a taxi,
tired from miles of mirrored hallways,
portraits of princes,
ceilings florid with winged cherubs.
We pass the giant Ferris wheel,
steel web of spokes and cables,
then parks with iron gates.
Behind them, headstones leaning.
Father starts to cry,
he wants to stop the car,
walk inside where
chestnut trees tower over wet grass,
place stones on the graves of Jews,
heavy, like his childhood there
where cobbled streets and carriages
are mixed up with memories
of the boys who beat him
outside the synagogue.
But mom stiffens,
doesn't want to hear his stories,
or see his tears,
commands the driver, "Go on!"
We three girls in the back seat
with our camel hair coats
and patent leather shoes
are the bargaining chip
they use against each other.
It's over in an instant.
What's left is his silence,
her headache,
our cries to stop for ice cream
at the next konditorei.

Beth Sholom

1.
Every Sabbath
a feeble looking man,
stooped over,
arrived after morning service
wearing a threadbare coat,
a rag of a jacket,
thick and oily brown
with patches coming undone.
We were all headed next door
to the big social hall
for the *Oneg Shabbat*
to sing songs and break bread.
At a long narrow table
he stuffed honey cakes
and almond cookies
into the deep chambers of his coat
until they bulged.
Then he'd wolf down *challah*
and gulp *Manischewitz*
from tiny Dixie cups laid out in neat rows.
I was scared of him,
called him *"Pockets,"*
gave him wide berth.
He was sometimes joined
by a small woman, half-crazy,
with short black curls,
a lazy eye and limp.
The two would quickly devour
what they could, then disappear
back to the streets where they lived.
The Rabbi welcomed them
and my father told me
they were angels,
God's emissaries,
who honored us by their visit.

2.
I had mixed feelings about this place.
Rabbi White frightened me;
he paced the pulpit like a caged lion
admonishing us to be better Jews.
Sometimes he'd spit as he spoke,
his passion mounting as he decried racism,
or exhorted women to have more babies.
The congregation was a hodgepodge—
poor emigres, local celebrities,
lost souls, political mucky-mucks
rubbing shoulders in their suits and skinny ties.
Sitting in the crowded sanctuary,
in the light of stained glass,
I gazed at them, bewildered,
a thick prayer book open in my lap.
Sometimes I ran down the central staircase
passing a small wood-lined chamber
where a *minyan* of Russian men with *tallit*
liked to pray in musty privacy.
I'd slip out from communal prayer,
go daydream by myself
in a cold concrete courtyard
where every autumn a fragile *Succah*
stood decorated in blue and white,
adorned with a *lulav* and *etrog,*
and sagging paper chains
that shivered in the wind.

West Portal

I knocked on Willie Mays' door,
mumbling "Trick or Treat,"
shy, in my terry-cloth tiger suit.
I was eight and he lived close by
after racists forced him
from the leafy neighborhood just blocks away.
His big hands ladled lolly-pops
into our paper bags, signed photos for us
on the front steps
while our knees knocked with excitement.

West Portal Elementary before busing,
stars and stripes hung high
in the auditorium where we recited the pledge
and waited in line for the polio vaccine,
sweet sugar cube on little pink tongues.
Day in, day out, air raid drills under wooden desks,
the bleak room where Miss Sangster scolded me
when I painted turquoise cubes
floating in space, instead of the pitcher with flowers.

Kids everywhere, our playground
a pandemonium of laughter, small fists
on tetherballs, steel chains
swinging as we flew higher, leaning
on leather strips, heads thrown back.
I wasn't athletic but I sometimes won at four-square,
and only grasped who I was one day
on the blazing asphalt when I beat Rosie
and she yelled in my face, "Dirty Jew!"

I never fit in, though Janie invited me over,
such a thrill, until she proudly pointed
to the dreadful crucifix dangling over her bed,
the frightening naked man
with spikes in painted flesh.
"You killed Jesus!" she whispered to me

with freaky glee, her green eyes
gleaming, the words blistering, thrashing
in my ears as I ran home, the candy gone sour.

Gun in the Closet

Smith & Wesson, gently resting
in a velvet-lined box
next to a souvenir boomerang,
engraved aboriginal artifact,
and grandma's pearls
held tight on a string.
A portent or inheritance,
tucked in a steel safe
inside a dim hallway closet,
Dad's revolver, waiting.
Mom doesn't like that firearm,
badgers him to get rid of it.
He won't listen.
One morning, a surge of excitement
and terror when he opens the safe,
grabs the gun, goes to find
the skunk in our basement,
small creature who makes her den
in the gravel behind rusted tools
and broken-down file cabinets,
clawing around in the dark,
keeping us up at night
for weeks on end.
Dad steps slowly, quietly,
fist clenched over the grip.
We three sisters beg him not to do it,
faces red, contorted, crying,
a pocket-sized Greek chorus swaying
in flannel pajamas at the top of the stairs.
It happens suddenly.
We hear the single shot
ring through the house,
inhale the spray, metallic,
sad odor of sulphur and wet fur
wafting through the house for days.

One Martini Please

We met in our basement clubhouse
the girls from the neighborhood
Kimmy, Lollie and Susie from across the crooked street,
and we sisters, Joanie and me
in stretch pants and dirty ankle socks
cross legged on the plywood floor,
creating the magazine we called "One Martini Please"
scratching and scribbling with Number Two pencils,
inhaling perfume of Pink Pearl erasers
rubbed and crumbling on thick white paper,
a hundred images of martini glasses and Barbies,
weekly booklets bound up with scotch tape and secrecy.
Upstairs mom in the kitchen
Cronkite on TV,
those days before we all went wild
and the girls got bras
and one belted her mom in the eye
and ran after her dad with an ax until
she locked her bedroom door
and the men from Langley Porter kicked it in
and took her away.
So many confidences kept.
The father who drank or came home smelling of
another woman's sweat, or the child
who heard voices that weren't there,
and the one whose torment lay
dormant for years
until let loose staring down the wide brim
at a skewered cocktail olive
floating over the slender glass stem.

Girl Scouts

An olive-green sash
draped over my budding breasts
every Tuesday after school,
drab slash over a khaki uniform,
its badges boasting *Housekeeping, Cooking, First Aid.*
Trained to keep the Promise,
serve God and country, respect authority,
be a sister to every Scout.
Proud of my *Photography* badge awarded
for what I shot with a new Polaroid.
I'd learned to thread a golden roll of Kodachrome
just like the sewing machine in Home Ec,
required for girls at school.
I was jubilant with those glossy images—
black and white squares
of girls pitching tents at summer camp,
eucalyptus trees in city fog,
our family's cat lying in repose
on my *India Imports* bedspread,
each shot neatly framed inside a white border.
But by the time our group leader
handed me the little round patch
I was sick of flag ceremonies and
reciting the Pledge. One day I came
home from the troupe, told my mother
it was over, what did she think
she was doing sending me
to Nazi training camp?

Forest Hill Station 7:00 am

Inside the tunnel buried
beneath the hill, walls of chalk tile,
shimmer of smoke and grime
stretching down the platform.
Light bulbs, bare, on thin wires
dangle low from the vaulted ceiling.
At midpoint, dull metal tracks,
rails littered with gravel,
candy wrappers skittering.
Down the line, shadows and damp air converge,
a man in loose trousers waits by an old wooden bench.
A single headlight emerges,
a miner's cart from an underground shaft.
The tram slows; flurry of black dust,
smell of stale oil.
The trolley rolls south
towards Twin Peaks passage,
passengers staring out the unwashed windows.

Red Skateboard

rolling over sidewalks wet
wind slapping my
face riding glazed
with mist speeding past
Ortega Noriega Moraga streets
clapboard houses eucalyptus trees
my narrow slice of wood on steel
wheels right foot
leading as I push back fast
each concrete crack a burning jolt
up my tensile spine
the big kids ahead
Ricky Susie Joey streaming
through the grid of pavement
my arms wide down park paths
ribbons unfurling
across the Great Highway salt
gusts of sand in eyes in teeth
in hair sweep of surfers on black
water pelicans sandpipers
campfires stretching down
a boundless coast

Urban Renewal

Urban Renewal

Pulverized pavement, glass,
a contagion of demolitions,
skeletal Victorians
and piles of mattresses on broken curbs.
On corners, families stand, silent,
bulldozers and pile drivers
breaking pipes, turning
earth upside down.
Pieces of hand painted signs,
words severed from clapboard,
hieroglyphs in the flinty landscape.
Through cordoned-off streets
Dad slowly maneuvers
our wood-paneled Rambler
to Mt. Zion,
despondent charity hospital
at neighborhood's edge,
a fault line deep as the San Andreas.
We hear the pounding
and drilling from the doctor's lounge
where he pours another cup of burnt coffee.
"Giving comfort and care to the needy"
words carved into the lintels
above emergency room doors.
I play hopscotch in a sterilized hallway.
Gurneys move in and out.
The backhoes and tractors keep up their work.

Human Be-In

She took me to the Be-In, mom's new friend,
happy, carefree woman holding my hand
as we strolled through the crush of stoned hippies,
rolling landscape of dancing girls, trampled daisies,
mongrel dogs wearing bandanas.
A bearded yogi handed me a flyer, bright purple,
with a big black spiral in the middle,
the jagged print reading "Turn On, Tune In, Drop Out."
An electric guitar was playing somewhere,
I could barely hear it amid the clamor
and closeness of bodies, pitched volume
of sunlight pouring down on us all.
When my mother's friend dropped me at home, she tried to
seduce mom in the kitchen; I was in my room
tacking the mutinous flyer to my bulletin board
beside class photos and carefully cut pictures
of Twiggy and Veruschka. Coffee and anarchy
percolated merrily, before the garage door creaked open
and my weary father pulled in.

Zig-Zags

The neighborhood gang ran
criss-cross through backyards,
tearing the stems of sourgrass,
sucking out the lemony sap,
plucking curbside nasturtiums
tasting the sweet pepper nectar.
We'd shake down from trees
little red bombs to throw at each other
until we were stained with their juice.
Sometimes we'd climb a snaking path to Hawk Hill
and look down on miles of tract homes,
silvery streets named for Spanish invaders,
paved over sand dunes stretching west.
On the rocky outcrop,
we'd roll joints with sticky pre-teen fingers,
Mendocino shake on Zig Zags,
a happy blue-bearded man
stamped on the cover
of the thin white papers
that we delicately licked shut.
I had a face full of pimples
and was the fattest of the group
certain I'd never go to a dance
though I still dreamt of love.
At twilight we'd walk down the winding trail
overgrown with purple ice plants,
cross sidewalks cracked from earthquakes,
smell the cool, wet lawns spread out
under a ceiling of fog.

The Poet's Party

Mom in a paisley dress fills the bathtub
with ice and amber bottles of beer when
the guests arrive, grinning
like Cheshire cats in black turtlenecks.
They sing, they spew, they spark
as I tip-toe room to room,
breathing in the bruised bouquet
of menthol smoke and day-old sweat.
Lamantia, ash from his cigarette
slowly burning a hole in our big bourgeois armchair,
Ruggles, stumbling, heaving on the front porch,
Gilbert and Gregg, curled together on the couch,
her hair a constellation of stars
orbiting voluptuous shoulders,
and Brautigan, a silent gargoyle
staring through me, the stripling
with braces and pigtails.
There are throngs of them,
away from their single room occupancies,
their studios, their lovers' beds,
crowded into our buttoned-down house.
This frightening, thrilling landscape of reckless desire,
an impossible city, now visible.

Literary Agent

She was very sexy.
That's what mom said
and I felt it too
when she visited us
after visiting him
at San Quentin.
She arrived at our house
in a miniskirt and heels,
raven hair and English accent,
our living room her confessional.
She was crazy for the locked-up revolutionary
and his dazzling letters,
the rough notes for *Soledad Brother.*
And stunning,
the ferocity of her passion,
the whole house trembling with her rapture
as she held my mother's hand and wept.
I was bewildered,
George Jackson in his cell,
the jackals circling,
my school friends with black berets
clutching copies of *Soul on Ice,*
prison yards and hidden pistols,
his brother in the courtroom
with a sawed-off shotgun,
sniper shots from a guard tower,
and the gorgeous visitor,
unconsolable
on our living room couch.

Mom On Fire

"I want to be alone" she said,
like Garbo in *Grand Hotel,* unreachable,
with a migraine, curtains closed,
under a mohair blanket, alone.
Which she was,

three times each week on the couch
with her therapist, burning,
like the quad where she stood
clutching a pen and notebook amid tear gas,
a riot of cops and clubs, thousands
of angry fists in the air
and Kay Boyle on a flatbed truck
shouting "Hayakawa-Eichmann!"

Home from school one night,
mom read a poem she'd written,
The Burning of the Birds,
Montezuma's plumed quetzals and ibises,
brilliant feathers, iridescent wings,
how they screamed
when Cortés laid them on his fire,
how the smoke rose
into the sky. I wanted to hide
under the kitchen table,
shaken by the animal holocaust she made
as real as the people
with numbers tattooed,
blue ink on pale flesh
flaking into flame—

not like her friend Abba, the Hebrew
phoenix, who rose
out of the Nazi inferno, swooping down
into our home twenty years after
the War to carry mom off
in his Partisan poet talons.

"Resist, resist to the last breath!"
he said to his comrades in the Vilna ghetto.
But she didn't. And soon she would leave
for the puzzlement of a foreign language,
words running backwards
like secret code, her
rapture transcendent, supernatural.

News

My transistor announces it.
Little box wrapped in black leather
held to my ear, bleeding static
into my tangled-up head.
A cavalcade of assassinations,
promotions for Pepsi, and *Hey Jude.*
The kids from school gather at Lisa's,
dance slow in each other's arms,
Otis Redding on the turntable,
silver stylus on the grooves
carving tiny wounds in our hearts.
We sit around a *Ouija* board,
fingers on a planchette gliding
over the marbled surface,
slipping off the edge. Oblivion.
Skyhawks and Dragonflies,
a squadron of newspaper images—
the naked girl in half-tone,
arms outstretched, running,
the young man in a cotton shirt
casually shot on a Saigon street.
I look up to the muddy sky
hoping to see a message in the stars
but see only zippered body bags
dropping from holes of transport planes
onto the stained tarmac.
Walter Cronkite reads the death count,
his face dissolving into black and white dust,
neon powder, napalm adrift.

Denise

Two kinky haired girls, comrades
running to the bathroom between classes,
smearing pink lipstick on puckered lips.
On the bus after school, binders on laps,
gossiping about boys and Smokey Robinson.
I'm off at the crest of the hill,
you ride down Parnassus,
descending to The Haight.
Confidantes who don't do sleepovers,
but we speak on the phone for hours
lying on our beds, doors closed
so our mothers won't hear.
After summer vacation
you come back with an Afro
and *The Autobiography of Malcolm X*.
I'm not sure what to say and
we don't speak about it but
I buy the Grove press paperback,
$1.25, block letters blood red,
his handsome furious face
and outstretched fist exploding
on the cover. My hands burn
clutching it in the long hallway,
past lines of steel lockers
and broken water fountains,
porcelain, dirty white like me. How can I
compete with your affection, your rapture
when he talks of *The Ballot or the Bullet?*
There he is, in Harlem, in Mecca, in Accra,
exultant, sublime. Denise you are leaving me,
By Any Means Necessary,
while he strides up to the podium
at the Audubon Ballroom,
and our friendship
fades to black.

Name Changes

Maybe it was the blood, lost virginity,
but I changed my name and can't remember
why. Or because my sister recast herself,
careening from girl to woman,
an identity that shifted—
the dancer became a dove, the dove a saint.
I can't remember the name of the movie
either, the one she took me to
slipping out, undiscovered by our parents
to Cedar Alley Cinema in a Tenderloin passageway.
They were showing something foreign,
Antonioni or Wojciech Has,
businessmen in sunglasses and sleek Armani suits,
racy women in spaghetti straps,
silver subtitles on a charcoal screen,
and a cat that roamed the narrow aisle.
There was the actor who changed his name too,
someone in the lead with an identity crisis.
We heard the whir of film rushing
past the sprockets
in the projection booth above our heads,
running all the way through the final credits
like a wild nitrate river.
Even the theater changed its name
and was soon forgotten,
like our old names
left behind in the dark.

Shoplifter

It was wrong,
but it was a thrill.
I did it with my girlfriends,
tough Lolitas from the Sunset,
not yet teens, old enough to know better.
Kris from Rivera Street,
Carla from Quintara,
leather wallet from an open purse at Playland,
cheap jewelry from the Stonestown Emporium,
my heart beating in my fingers,
the same that played
as I sat on the piano bench
with Mr. Jaffe practicing scales
later the same day.

Kris and her Irish mom had a pastel flat
bathed in a haze of cigarette smoke
and ocean fog. We sat close together
on the couch watching black and white TV,
drove to Reno one weekend,
walked over the shimmering concrete to Foster Freeze,
licked our soft vanillas in the dry heat.
At night her mom drank with a boyfriend in room number 6
while Kris and I, in string bikinis, splashed
and played. The motel pool was neon green
under the desert stars, and in the water,
we spoke of UFOs with strange older guys
who looked at us with longing, but dared not touch.

Next summer, a car crash, Kris was killed.
Carla moved to an apartment, bare
except for a bowl of oranges
and wall to wall carpet. I left the city,
thinking of the silvery streetcar tracks
we used to take to the rink by the beach;
skating with these girls,
our fantasies of Peggy Fleming

in chartreuse chiffon,
the sound of sharp blades cutting the surface
as we screamed with delight,
gliding past each other in circles,
listening to Motown, faster, faster.

The Back Room

It was behind the kitchen,
the corner with windows facing east,
small nook built for maids or nannies
of a by-gone time,
until the 60's, when my sister
moved in with our guinea pigs,
cages filled with sawdust
and flaccid lettuce leaves.
She taped psychedelic posters on the walls,
painted spider webs on the window shades
put on a black turtleneck
and stopped talking
right before she fastened the lock shut.
Days later, the men in white came,
kicked the door from its frame
and sent me in, first responder child,
to find her there
behind the hinges,
curled up teen with shiny hair
like the little creatures
softly squealing beside her.
I stood in that doorway not long after
the room now white-washed, bleached clean,
notebooks askew and reams of paper,
mom at a desk, back turned away
pounding on an electric typewriter
her hands hammering keys,
long fingers with their clean, mechanical tapping.

War of Attrition

Joanie's dragging plastic irrigation pipes
around date palms in the Negev.
I'm rolling joints in San Francisco
sewing them into the hem of my dress
to smuggle through customs
for us to smoke on the kibbutz.
It's what sisters do for each other.

Spring break, I fly over the ocean,
find her in the rocky desert,
sagebrush growing from hard soil
south of the prison and nuclear reactor.
We talk about an end to war
in this bleached out space,
paint pictures of camels and thistles,
acacia and wadis under the sun.

One night in the clapboard bungalow,
sitting on an army cot, she plays guitar—
Dylan, Buffy St. Marie.
Out of nowhere, strange whistles,
Phantoms sear across the violet sky,
thud and blast of missiles,
chaotic, guttural shouting as we scramble
in the dark to a shelter carved from rock
and dirt, crouching in the din until daybreak,
when we go back to the palm trees
as if it's normal,
hauling pipe in the morning.

We Board the 6 Masonic

Last class over, we board the 6 Masonic,
Linda, Laura and me with our book bags,
minds a mess of Hendrix and Nixon.
The streetcar slides down the hill,
black lace cables swinging wide overhead.
Around the corner, the man
in the plate glass window at Pasquale's
tosses the dough up high;
pizza mandalas spin on Irving Street.
Pregnant women cross the road
blown by a cold ocean wind,
disappear through revolving hospital doors
into neon waiting rooms.
A blaze of chalk bright Victorians,
Frederick, Masonic, Haight,
three ambrosial girls jump out,
beads swinging in sandalwood mist
all the way to the 'Psychedelic Shop'
where I sit on a hippie's corduroy lap as he
puts a sequin *bindi* on my forehead
and a sugary square of acid
on my teenage tongue.

Deep Red World

Privilege

Mattie's in all the birthday pictures,
wearing cateye glasses with rhinestones,
a big brown woman carrying a sheet cake with candles
to a table of little white girls in party dresses.
She gives me a delicate porcelain pony,
a present I proudly display on my bedroom shelf
taking her generosity for granted.
One day she disappears from the small back room
where she lived with us half the time,
taking her pillows and rose scented hand lotion with her.
I hear my parents whisper the word "cancer,"
but don't know what that is,
find my mother weeping in the kitchen.
Soon after, Mary arrives, holds me on her lap
to play pat-a-cake on the porch,
pushes the swing at the playground
in a crisply ironed dress, sometimes wears
a pretty scarf tied at the back of her neck,
covering hair that's soft and frizzy like mine.
She goes home to her family each night; I don't ask
who they are or where they live.
Mary knows where everything is in our house, and
how to hold the broom like a dance partner
as she sweeps the crumbs off the linoleum,
and how to hide a bottle of gin
behind the Clorox. I don't know why but
she too leaves us and then there's Fran,
a small German girl who comes every Friday promptly at 9,
sighing as she arrives at the front door,
blond hair straight and stringy.
When she heads to the laundry carrying a heavy basket,
my parents talk behind a closed door
about her sick husband, a pregnant teenage daughter.
When I start middle school my new friends
talk about revolution and make nasty jokes
about my privilege. My shame is a lead blanket;
I drag it around everywhere,

a toxic cape that trails on the floor.
And then I grow up, get pregnant,
and with mortification hire Laura,
the punk DJ at KALX radio,
to clean my house, and she tells me
not to sweat it, and so do her friends
Ngisti and Aklasia, who come from Eritrea
where they killed enemy soldiers
in their war of liberation before
coming to America where they now
wash my floor and don't care about my guilt.
Which is a privilege.

Cathy

You wore a trench-coat, belt tied,
pony-tail down your back like
your sable-haired sister who had polio,
wooden crutches, and straight A's.
Your birth mother Korean,
your dad a GI carrying you both
back to his wide-eyed wife, stateside,
where she raised you two with tenderness
after he walked out one day. An American story
you shared with me when we met in leotards
and tights in dance class stretching
and purling to *Sketches of Spain*.
Sometimes you'd pick me up
in your mom's rusting station wagon;
we'd roll down the windows,
play the radio so loud people would glare,
shake their heads with annoyance
as we drove around Lake Merced
where crusty old men were fishing for perch
and trout that burst with methylmercury.
After school, we'd return
to the tiny home your mom kept so clean,
and listen with unending devotion
to Joni Mitchell, the album
we couldn't live without that spring
when Nixon invaded Cambodia and the National Guard
gunned down students and the afternoon sun
spilled through the slats of worn-out window blinds
as we lay in the mesh of their shadows.

The Boys from the Haight

I laughed with the boys from the Haight;
we'd roll joints on the floor,
talk about Vietnam,
where to meet up at the next moratorium.
John signed my yearbook
with a funny looking hammer and sickle,
drafted me into the YSA
with a red pen and toothy grin.
We marched together in a big peace protest
down the center of the street
angry about idiots and fascists,
got rowdy on streetcars,
mostly joking, way too loud,
carousing with bookbags and lunchboxes,
all the way to Robert's Victorian
where we practiced slow dancing under a gabled roof
when his parents weren't home.
I learned the back roads south of the city
after school with David
driving along the San Andreas Fault
all the way to La Honda
through madrone and manzanita,
winding around those redwood hills
dreaming about longer journeys.
All before David became a seaman
writing love songs from Isla Mujeres,
before he lost his way and his letters
became a strange soup of poetry and incoherence,
then stopped arriving altogether.
Before John's brother was ambushed in Nicaragua,
shot dead while bringing electricity to farmers
and John moved to Oregon.
Before I lost touch with Robert
and the rest of the boys from the Haight,
everyone cast out,
scattering like we once did
when the cops fired tear-gas into the crowd.

N Judah to The Surf

Riding past stucco row houses,
Cantonese restaurants, neon signs at dusk.
Sagging phone lines, tangled web of overhead wire,
rumble of wheels turning on iron tracks.
Foghorns breathe all the way
to the last stop on the line
near the old horse stables. I step out
into the sharp switch of wind,
smell myrrh and sea salt,
smoke from beach bonfires
that cuts through my hair.
At a sheltering booth, Spanish tiles
in three shades of green, coiled rolls
of paper tickets. The marquee flickers,
little gold bulbs pulse like church candles
beside an altar, and I hear the waves
crashing on sand.

Om Shanti

The divine was everywhere—
In Precita Park, where hippie dervishes wore billowing skirts,
dancing, euphoric, arms linked across a vast meadow
beside the Army Street projects.
Amid the stately palms on Dolores, in a Queen Anne mansion
where scrawny men with beards taught us Kundalini
and how to sing mantras as we sat on hard pillows
with our legs twisted and aching.
Inside the House of Love and Prayer,
shabby wooden shack for lost Jewish kids,
where we sang a *niggun* on the floor,
and Rabbi Carlebach leaned into me,
put his greasy lips on mine,
his awful tongue in my mouth.
So many of us stoned kids in ragged bell-bottoms
roaming around the city
and God's messengers to show us the way.

Home Improvement

It was a year of fennel and shallots.
The kitchen was mom's European adventure
before her first flight across the Atlantic.
She went from meatloaf
to Boeuf Bourguignon, pouring red wine
with abandon into a cast iron casserole
spattered with gravy and desire, her mind adrift,
far from the Pyrex measuring cups and Fiesta ware.

She'd sometimes take me to happenings;
we'd lie on daybeds covered with Persian rugs
gaze at a staircase going nowhere,
and mobius strips in bold frames,
Escher at the Vorpal Gallery
until they ran out of sweet chardonnay.
Intoxicated, dizzy with possibility,
she brought home Hopi Kachina dolls,
lithographs by local artists,
a French watercolor picked up from an auction house.
She covered the walls up to the ceiling,
erotic shapes, impasto laid down with a knife,
an eight-foot canvas with thick strokes of orange and green
that made us all titter.

The doors and windows blew open,
no going back to the old order.
The household tumbled into jubilant anarchy,
one by one appliances broke down,
electric cords fell from their sockets.
The switch was on.
She was in no mood
for home improvement.

They Shoot Horses, Don't They?

Mom has taken me to the movies again.
We pass salted popcorn back and forth
in crushed velvet seats watching
people throw pennies at sailors,
farm workers, pregnant women.
A Depression era band plays *Easy Come, Easy Go*
in a seedy beach-town ballroom
while tired couples drag each other to and fro,
famished and fading through the late hours
of a dance marathon.
Jane Fonda smokes a cigarette in a frayed red dress;
one man's heart stops;
he drops to the grimy dancehall floor.
A woman in a loose kimono flips out;
men in white suits carry her away.
The MC, awash in sweat and stale gin,
yells "Yowza! Yowza!" into a blaring microphone.
Misery drifts down from the screen
into my anxious teenage lap.
Fonda, exhausted, stands at the shore,
unlocks the clasp on her little black purse
and delicately lifts a revolver.
My bag of popcorn, empty, crumpled, falls to the floor.
After the closing credits, we drive home,
Mom at the wheel, in the shadows of winding streets,
the rear-view mirror casting chimera,
silent specters from her past,
the dance lessons of her childhood,
where working class girls wore worn out slippers
on the polished oak floor,
the thin screen door of her parents' Seattle bungalow
where hobos would stand on the back porch, hungry,
while her mom made them sandwiches.
Decades after the Depression
Mom's sad face turns towards me,
as the city sirens drone
like a distant dancehall song.

Laura

When you got your driver's permit
you scribbled a letter to me
on yellow note paper
pressing down with bold exclamation marks,
crude drawings of smiling daisies
and little penciled fireworks.
You wrote you were celebrating this moment
reading *Native Son* in the bathtub, upstairs
in the North Beach apartment
where your family lived
and you wanted to tell me
you loved me.
The boys at school tried to get close
but we were happy to brush them off,
let our hair grow wild, wear long flowing skirts,
hitch a ride with strangers in a painted van
through the rainbow tunnel.
At your family's Christmas party we got high
and stood on the fire escape,
arms entwined, laughing at the kitschy pink lights
strung across rooftops all the way to the wharf,
telling each other these holidays were *bourgeois*.
And when we graduated,
you drove up to the mountains
with no forwarding address
and I never saw you again.

Mt. Lassen

Your parents drove us to the ancient volcano,
southern crater of the Cascades.
A week of treks along steep ravines
and creeks, lava beds of rock and ash,
through meadows erupting with fireweed,
and Indian paintbrush.
Eating pancakes with syrup,
rowing to the lake's far side,
lounging on a ramshackle deck
until mosquitos drove us indoors.
One night we made off in the dark,
pine needles underfoot, scent of bay leaves,
supple girls, and two older boys from a nearby cabin,
names we didn't know,
finally reaching an abandoned shack
where we climbed into two old cots,
rocking under eaves, all night
into the deep red world.
The next morning we said nothing of it.
It was still early,
I stood silent, watched from the window
as you walked to the water,
lay down on a wooden pier
leaning into the swells,
washing your long hair, slowly,
as it rippled in the shoals.

Steady

Conga drums and a guitar case filled with weed,
neat ounces in plastic bags you weighed with precision,
brought to school and sold by the football field.
Every day after classes your mom still at work
we slid onto the mattress on your bedroom floor
your long hair in my face, smooth soccer legs tangled
with mine, I'd nip the seashell you wore
on leather around your neck, that choker
emerging now from the only photo I have of you.

Part Slovenian, maybe in your cheekbones
or thighs, like Rodin's bronze *Thinker* we used
to sit under, near Land's End wet in thick fog.
You made your deals with stoners behind the bleachers,
worked hard on weekends painting houses,
took breaks on somebody's lawn, head thrown back in sunlight,
smiling and sipping beer, before I left for college and you
drove north, and the dark distance grew,
a shadow forest of giant sequoias, loamy, timeless.

At our high school reunion, your twin brother, the boy
with the strawberry birthmark who listened
from his room next door to our raw teenage sex, told me
things didn't go well for you, desolation and a cabin
in the land of permanent eclipse,
and there I was at the Irish Cultural Club
with two hundred strangers I thought I knew
and a small tumbler of something cheap, burning over ice.

Kelly Girl

I wore that short dress,
snap buttons and macramé belt,
filled in forms at Kelly Girl Temps,
landed it. First job,
60 words-per-minute on Geary Street,
insurance investigators—a smoky warehouse of men
in polyester, rotary phones, thicket of vulgar jokes,
and cramped room with girls wearing earphones
pounding away on IBM Selectrics.
Mr. Teeling called me into his office, the door
closed. A long silence, a strange look,
then, "Do you want to work weekends?"
My heart beating. At five o'clock
I was on a street smeared with blinking
martini glasses, a palette of neon
gold and bloody red, murky taprooms
with names like O'Keefe's, Tippy's,
The Bitter End, which it seemed like when
I finally got on a crowded bus
and a smelly guy sat down next to me
and began to masturbate.
I had to crawl over his wet hands
and fat lap to get out and
still have to keep trying to forget
his rough, flushed face.

Mug shot

The girl is sullen,
lips pursed, shaggy hair,
eyes dark lakes of revolt
burning through the photographer's lens.
She wears an old cowboy shirt,
pearly snaps unfastened, red rose in full bloom
embroidered above her heart, petals aflame.
How she loved that western chemise,
its hint of wild mustangs, Santa Ana winds.
How she turned her head skyward
as they held her arms behind her back,
dragged her down the stairs,
tore the sleeve from its seams.
How they clumsily thrust that blouse
into a plastic bag, threw it on a musty shelf
where it was lost forever.

Dream of the Stormy Petrel

1
We walk the midnight streets tripping,
long hair, frayed jeans, teenagers
ending up in a booth at a 24-hour diner.
Inside the red vinyl dreamscape, apple pie,
a smiling waiter, the radio blaring Aretha.
A neon sign in the window blinks *"Open,"*
like Cyrillic, some Soviet message beamed
down on us from outer space.
Outside, foghorns, a river of cars
accelerating onto the freeway, heading south
under a constellation of lampposts.

2
Glenn and I drive east over the old steel span.
We swallow a square of blotter acid
kept cool in a Berkeley refrigerator,
walk the south side streets after dark,
sit on a curb outside the Roxie Mart.
Dwight Way dances in spectacular color,
the glint of a car's fenders a secret directive.
At dawn we head back to our faded bungalow,
the hand me down couch, stereo speakers
and woofers blasting Bowie.
All around us tattered artifacts, sad appliances,
each object weeping gorgeous proletarian opera.

3
In Santa Cruz there's a hill
overlooking the molten sea.
You perch on the edge of a crag,
every particle in your being
illuminated. Flares of the sun fuse you
to molecules of air and ocean spray
and you see the stormy petrel, *a streak of sable
lightning* bursting from an old Russian poem
lodged deep within your chest.

Divorce

1.
Our parents called us into the hopeless kitchen,
sat us down at the empty table.
There was a terrible quiet.

She said she was leaving.
He began to cry.
We left the table one by one.

I went to my room, shut the door.
On my knees, nothing
but stillness. Outside the window,
leaves were falling.

I saw a mountain of suitcases
piled up on the sidewalk.
She was in a suede jacket, waiting for a taxi;
I couldn't make out her expression.

He stayed in his bathrobe, wandering
around the house. His worn out slippers
made a chirring sound on the floor.

After that it was winter.
I drove down Highway 1,
the tank close to empty.

In the hard rain, a stretch of coastal road
had collapsed into the sea,
a 'slip out,' causing a deep cleft.
The downpour continued.

2.
The taxi sped to the international terminal.
A long flight, some cursory
questions at passport control.
Under the scorching Levantine sun, my mother slipped

into her new life with the volatile professor,
Clark Gable of the Judean hills, scotch at the ready,
the man who could finally see who she was.

My father fell in with a war refugee,
a Berliner in a black negligee, escaped
prisoner from a concentration camp,
whose coke-bottle glasses and *Taittinger Brut*
blurred her castaway past.

They moved on. I was buried
in the shards left behind,
the rupture of divorce
diminished for a time
by my teenage attraction
to a boy from Beverly Hills.
I wanted to be possessed.
He was willing.

Numb in the tide of transit
from one parent to another,
one continent to another,
my ghost limbs tried to paddle
in the undercurrent.

3.
Through turbid waters,
I could barely make out
the bottom of the sea,

the place where sediment drifts
down into a sandy bed.

A hazy detachment,
vertigo, as my step-mother
struggled to charm me
at the first holiday dinner
after the split.
Leek and potato soup. Poached halibut.
Everything was woozy white.

My irritable step-dad
went the opposite route,
the veins in his neck throbbing
as he tried to choke back
his displeasure with my restive visits
to his Holy Land.

The old neighborhood was now a foreign ruin.
What had been casual, familiar,
West Portal, the Inner Sunset,
became my private site of pilgrimage,
a once-a-year visit on the way to the cemetery.
The front lawns and photo albums,
upward mobility and post-war optimism
became an indifferent landscape,
temples and tombs of stucco and cement,
shrines and sacred places
detached from history.

Homecoming

Sisters

There's a photo of us,
a creased Polaroid,
white borders dissolving
into surf on jagged rocks
below, as we balance
on the rim of Mt. Tam, reckless
teens, arms outstretched
in a blast of wind, wild hair
pell-mell, indiscriminate.
Sharon in a wool pea-coat
buttoned tight over her perfect
ballerina body,
Joan wrapped in a Greek
fisherman sweater, dark
curls floating about her face.
And me, long legs, patched denim.
We're on the brink
of something big, about to break
out of that silver print chrysalis—
the next frame is empty as if
we've fallen off that hillside
into the cold coastal flurry.
But we'd only turned, heading back
to the car we'd left
on a rough gravel road.
We took off down the mountain,
not speaking to one another,
Curtis Mayfield on a tinny car radio,
and a chorus of stones
crunching under steel belted tires,
our shared story beginning to unravel
as we turned the bend,
pebbles scattering everywhere.

Homecoming

Orange blossom and sulphur—
you get off the plane and smell it.
Steam of the coastal plain
blowing in through taxi windows,
radio blaring Ofra Haza and news updates.
You snake up the mountain
past burnt jeeps, desiccated cactus.
Bleached stone markers on hillsides
silently welcome you back.

What is homecoming?
Mom in the kitchen chopping dill
for cold cucumber soup. She ladles it
into ceramic bowls on Rashba,
the leafy street named for a medieval rabbi.
You dream in the ruins of this city,
on the winding path under pine and jacaranda
past parking lots and ancient tombs,
through summer days in the tile library, nights outdoors
listening to Yehudit Ravitz sing bossa nova,
and Yehuda Poliker's bouzouki-laced riffs.

You hitch a ride to Gaza just an hour away,
visit a Quaker kindergarten and eat fresh fish
in Mary's kitchen—Marx, Gandhi and Arafat
stirred up into one dusty mess.
Return to King David street and sit on a curb
smoking a cigarette that stinks like an Israeli jail.

Friday mornings you go to the market where
they're plucking feathers, warming pita,
hawking pickles and halva and dates
and your plastic sack is heavy with melon
and Iraqi eggplant and sesame pastries.
In between Ottoman archways,
young men with dark glasses
prowl around, Uzis slung over their shoulders.
You don't feel safe.

All the cousins and friends want you to stay.
For the holidays and picnics under olive trees,
for the work you'll do together and the protests you'll go to,
and the film festivals at King Solomon's pools, and the babies
and the bombings, and the funerals
and the settlers and their prayers
and the angry boys at soccer games
screaming like Nazis in a Jerusalem stadium.

October War

Dry wind, thistles knee high, little razor pricks
as I tramp through fields on a morning hike
until the sirens blast, then breathless, race back
to where mom pours water in the tub,
spreads masking tape on the windows,
cross-hatched, to stave off shattered glass.
We scramble to the corner market for cookies
and cigarettes, meager care packages
we'll send to boy-soldiers on the front
when there's nothing left to do.
In the evening, shades shut tight,
a blackout to confuse the enemy.
On a crackling broadcast, the King across the border
announces our demise through static:
"Victorious armies have stormed the country!"
But it's not real. Of this I'm certain—
the sound of helicopters overhead,
the patriotic speeches of the generals,
women wearing black at the pharmacy,
the strange truth of a city emptied of men.
I smell the *mujadra* mom cooks in the afternoon,
absently adjusting the flames on the burners,
waiting for this to be over.
Stir-crazy one day, she drives madly to the front
with a lemon cake for Bill; returns home silent, dusty,
shuts the bedroom door.
There's a place called the Valley of Tears,
where everyone in Danny's tank
is blown to bits, except for Danny
who crawls out, body half-burned.
Rachel is pale, spectral as she speaks of him
in our darkened living room, blue eyes covered
by a veil of unkempt hair.

Jealous

I was madly jealous.
Her raven hair always lustrous,
almond eyes pools of topaz,
how she could wear a loose paisley blouse
over her smooth body.
Hiding together under the dining room table
reading Dr. Seuss, her supple legs
crossed mine with perfect grace.
We'd lie together and giggle
at the Hindu puppet gods,
the fantastic Bohemian décor her parents hung
from the ceiling, run upstairs
to her mom's jewelry box,
scavenge necklaces and earrings
for our dress-up fantasies,
Russian ballerinas or Flamenco dancers.
Downstairs, her three older sisters left guitars
and dulcimers resting on big pillows
scattered across the living room floor
beneath a giant Modigliani nude
with a long, doe-like neck.
It was all heavenly, my envy knew no bounds,
and every time I visited,
her oldest sister would run her gentle finger
across my baby fat cheek, purring,
calling me 'Little Peach Fuzz,'
making me dizzy with joy.
And then they all picked up and moved to Israel,
gorgeous hippy family now with peace placards
and doves at some desert protest against the Occupation,
and one day, in Jerusalem, the oldest sister,
on her way to summer school class, boarded a bus
that was blown up by a young freedom fighter,
shrapnel flying everywhere,
and I heard the family had to collect
the pieces at the morgue.

Phantom

        The ghost hovers over the room,
her low voice following me
ever since that first sighting
when she appeared on TV
in a film about the Summer of Love.
She was there in the Park,
in the crowd that spread like smoke
across the Polo Field,
smiling and flickering inside
our cathode ray Zenith.
I took a polaroid of that image, pinned it
to the cork board in our kitchen
next to Fannie Lou Hamer
and Patti Smith. But
maybe it wasn't her.
Just a private delusion.
        The specter re-appeared
in newsprint photos, halftone
images where she pouted
under French bangs. Was that really her
or Anna Karina in *Band of Outsiders?*
Odile in a black sweater, line-dancing,
snapping her fingers to the beat.
        Once I saw her in a dream,
across the ocean, lying in bed wearing
a red silk nightgown with spaghetti straps,
three daughters by her side
as she slid from consciousness
into the milky sheets.
        And yesterday she flew through my window,
filament of moisture from an atmospheric river.
There was laughter all around
as she opened a small cedar box
to let white doves fly,
wings outstretched over desert sand.

Braids

Fridays I'd sift flour
into a ceramic bowl.
She kneaded, then
placed the soft dough
in the sunlight,
covered it with a dishcloth
and let it rise.

I wanted to help her make braids
out of the batter—
three ends stuck together
coiled up in a buttery embrace.
She let me paint it
with a stiff brush,
Renoir girl with golden yolk,
and we'd drizzle poppy seeds
on the glossy surface
of the steaming loaf.

"Three sisters," she'd say
pulling at our curls
in front of the bathroom mirror,
Sharon loaded up with rollers and *Dippity-Do,*
Joan with a wild ponytail,
and me with tangled vines,
thick strands for pig tails
"Braid them tight!"

In Jerusalem, years later,
a student came to her door every Friday
selling wildflowers from a plastic bucket.
She'd smile with delight,
cut the stems just so,
put them in a copper pot
on the coffee table
before the evening blessings
over the wine and twisted challah.

Daisies, iris, thistle,
and Sabbath prayers,
before she forgot the names of the blossoms
or the eggs boiling on the stove
or where she put her passport.

Sometimes we'd go out
to a grill with arched ceilings and pale tile floors
for a meal of fish with cumin and za'atar.
The place was loud, filled with Jews and Arabs
eating together and laughing.
She introduced me as her sister,
our tanned arms braided together.
Those lovely dinners
before everything unraveled,
the pleasure we had together
until a bomb exploded there,
until her memory slipped away.

The Land of Forgetfulness

>*Shall Thy wonders be known in the dark?*
>*And Thy righteousness in the land of forgetfulness?*
>   —*Psalm 88: 13*

Song of faith
or despair, a psalm,
a Bach cantata,
a verse that ends in darkness.
Which is worse:
to forget
or to be forgotten?
Mom rests, the doors of the memory unit
shut tight. She sits at the window
looking out at two redwoods.
They extend beyond the frame of glass,
out of reach. The landscape narrows
as we nestle together
on a love-seat,
next to a row of potted bromeliads,
long-lasting, forgiving.
Even the tea in our cups
condenses into steam.

On Her Desk

An Egyptian scarab,
flaking, fading.
A small silver swan,
and one dark stone, smooth.
Three paperweights
of unknown origin
perhaps acquired in a museum shop,
or a gift from a dying friend.
Maybe found near a mountain stream
where she first felt him next to her.
Resting for years on her old teak desk.
These totems are mute, enigmatic,
exquisite, can't answer
my questions about the past,
about the power they conferred,
or her impenetrable choices.
Or was it
she was simply drawn
to the graceful beauty
of these humble possessions
and their functional weight
residing on stacks of paper
next to a perfectly round
red lacquer bowl.

Purple Heels

For Chana B.

I pull the lid off slowly,
fold back the tissue paper,
a coy strip tease,
delicately lift them out of their cardboard box,
unveiling my first pair—
periwinkle, a slim ribbon at the ankle,
heels high as heaven.
They're luscious like a cheap romance novel,
proudly purchased with the earnings
of my weekly allowance,
sublime.

Mom clenches her teeth, aghast,
but her friend, the young professor
visiting for tea, winks at me,
a secret communication shared
on the living room couch
while mom has turned away.
She's sly, this red-haired teacher,
eminent writer, survivor of a reeling
vertigo felt after her husband vanished
into the white-washed wards. Lost
like the words he translated
from an ancient manuscript,
parchment crumbling to dust.
The *Song of Songs* running backwards,
a sorrow I understand even as a young girl.

In the year of tumors and scans
we meet in a crowded waiting room,
talk of those brazen shoes,
color of orchid, wild lavender,
ripe plums bursting with life.
Her smooth head is wrapped in silk,
she moves with a weary limp.

We go to a friend's lecture—
Freud's Jewish dream, feminism,
the salty mother tongue, all stirred together.
She leans into me as we enter the auditorium,
settle into folding chairs.
Her cane lies on the floor between us,
a question mark,
a serpentine smile.

Return

Out the cabin window a bank of fog
loosened from its holding pattern
along the Pacific. Clouds spilled
over western hills; the jet
descended onto SFO's runway.
Freeway off-ramps pulsed
towards old haunts—Red's Place,
The Rite Spot, La Rondalla.
My roots dug deep in the concrete terrain.
Memories of San Bruno jail, two weeks
in solitary reading Ho Chi Minh,
mounds of sedge grass growing wild
outside thick plate windows.
The party with Friends of the Filipino People
after release. A mess of us in Doc Martens
dancing to Grandmaster Flash, the smoke
in the alley outside The Roxie
before *Ashes and Diamonds.*
And when Robert was wasting
and David disintegrated at SF General,
delirious, strapped to the gurney,
ferried to lock-down, face turning sepia,
he gripped my outstretched hand
and then let go.

After the End of the World

1.
A bed, a window, sterile gloves.
Friends, spectral, lay
prostrate on hospital sheets.
Curt Robert David Dean.
The green line flattens,
they disappear like chalk
outlines on asphalt
after it rains.

2.
Mom wears her gas mask like a purse
strung over her shoulder,
stylish and brown,
with its neat little clasp.
She takes it to the symphony
in Jerusalem during the war.
The orchestra keeps playing
while the sirens go off
and Scuds explode nearby
shaking the concert hall.
"You get used to it," she says.

3.
I make scoops of ice cream out of Play-doh,
lumpy blue balls with red pins sticking out.
Deniz and I drop them into little plastic cones
"More sprinkles!" he squeals with joy.
The fleshy spheres look like
the virus in our living room.
Afterwards, we wash hands at the kitchen
sink and watch thin soapy bubbles
spiral down the drain.

Formica Table

Formica table in the kitchen,
color of cracked ice,
chrome legs a double helix,
matching vinyl chairs.
Each evening a performance
of pot roast and carrots—
Dad, bone-tired at the head,
Mom at the opposite end,
shape-shifting in a fire-blue dress.
After dessert, they argue about Vietnam,
sniper fire over the rims of coffee cups.
And I'm there too, invisible,
lost on the far side of the laminate.

Years later, this table is covered with the grime
of bachelor parties, take-out dinners,
red coronas from last night's wine.
Adam fills a plastic basket with soiled towels
and sheets, sweats and socks.
He carries that load to the corner laundromat,
and when he returns, he clears the table,
folds his linens on the cool, grey surface
that looks to him like smoke, spilled sugar,
frost on the windowsill.

A piece of furniture like this moves around
from one family member to another.
Once modern, now retro, evidence of excess
or contempt, traces of desire
or heartache hardly score its surface.
Now in Samia's dining room
laden with ceramic platters,
hummus and tahina, pitchers of masala chai.
Someone is strumming a saz,
young women with henna on their hands,
hamsas round their necks,
divorce on their minds, converse

around the melamine. The clamor of voices,
their restless lives, layers of resin,
opaline, sealing the mid-century core.

Burial

It should have been on a hill, overlooking
the desiccated pines of Bet Shemesh.
A desire she made clear to us half way around the world.
She wanted to lie down there, the sun beating
the terraced landscape with its pottery shards
and ancient Canaanite bones,
with its Kings and Prophets, and her dear friends.
But it was too late, she was here, not there
and we chose the rose-colored
stone, American granite,
the one called *Paradiso*
as if she were Dante's Beatrice,
luminous in a draped gown,
guiding us through the afterlife,
like the Gustave Doré illustrations
she gazed at lovingly, in her pajamas,
serene and vacant,
inside the memory center, *The Divine Comedy*
open in her lap, slowly turning the pages.
We had the grave cutter carve three names—
the one given by her father and mother,
the one that people knew her by,
the one she acquired for herself,
etched above the Hebrew inscription
and the dates of her birth and death.
And we stood in the wet grass
looking down at the daisies,
so prolific and improbable, growing
where there should have been cracked earth.

Notes

Literary Agent
    The literary agent was Mary Clemmey, the British literary agent for George Jackson, Bishop Tutu and others.

Mom on Fire
    "Abba" was Abba Kovner, one of the great poets of Israel; a Lithuanian partisan leader during WWII, famous for his Vilna Ghetto manifesto "Let us not go like lambs to the slaughter."

War of Attrition
    Large scale raids, shelling, and airstrikes between Israel and Egypt, Jordan and their allies, 1967-1970.

The Boys From the Haight
    YSA—Young Socialist Alliance

N Judah to The Surf
    The Surf Theater was the preeminent San Francisco movie house screening foreign, art, and independent cinema until it closed in 1985.

October War
    Also known as the Yom Kippur War, the 1973 Arab-Israeli war.

About the Author

Deborah Kaufman was born and raised in San Francisco. She was founding Director of the San Francisco Jewish Film Festival before becoming an award-winning documentary filmmaker. This is her first collection of poetry.

www.ingramcontent.com/pod-product-compliance
Lightning Source LLC
Chambersburg PA
CBHW031124160426
43192CB00008B/1107